The BLUE Game

written by Jenny Alexander
illustrated by Tom Clayton

Chapter One

What About Me?

Not long after Sam moved into the new flat, her mother started looking for a job. She bought the local paper every day, and drew rings around the jobs she was interested in.

Sam noticed that a lot of them involved working in the evenings or at weekends. She was angry. Nobody had asked her what she thought about it, just like nobody had asked her how she felt about moving into a new flat.

"What about me?" she demanded one day.

Mrs Summerday was about to put a ring around an advertisement for waitresses at a new restaurant in the High Street.

She looked up in surprise. “What do you mean, what about you?” she asked.

Sam frowned at her. “What if I don’t want you to get a job?”

Her mother sighed. “I’m afraid you haven’t got much choice,” she said. “We need the money.”

She went back to studying the paper. Sam looked over her shoulder. She watched her mother draw a ring around The Garden Restaurant advertisement.

"What's going to happen to me if you go out to work in the evenings?" Sam protested.

"You'll just spend more time with Dad," said her mum, not looking up.

"But what about when he's on night shift?" said Sam.

Mrs Summerday looked up, irritably. “For heaven’s sake!” she snapped. “Give me a break, will you? I haven’t even got a job yet. And at this rate, I probably never will.”

They both glanced at the pile of rejection letters on the work surface. Mrs Summerday had been writing application letters and making phone calls for weeks, and she hadn’t even got an interview.

But Sam wouldn’t let it go. “Well?” she said.

“Well, if Dad and I are both at work, you can go to a friend’s house. Okay?”

Sam thought about it. Mouse and Jojo's was like a madhouse half the time, with Pip and his friends getting into all kinds of mischief. Ben's house was full of Tessa's dreadful music. Sam liked some quiet time for reading in the evenings. Donut's house was quieter, but she'd probably die of homemade cake poisoning if she had to spend much time there.

"No. It isn't okay to go to a friend's house," said Sam.

"Well it's just going to have to be," said her mum, finally.

Chapter Two

Grumbles with Mrs Green

Sam felt hard done by all the next day, and she was still in a bad mood when she went to take Scrap for a walk.

Mrs Green invited her in for a cup of tea afterwards, but even a slice of her delicious strawberry tart didn't make Sam feel any better.

"You look as if you've lost a pound and found a penny," said Mrs Green. "What's wrong?"

Sam gave a heavy sigh. "My mum's getting a job," she said. She realised that it didn't sound like much of a big deal. "She didn't ask me," she explained. "And when I told her I didn't want her to, she just said it was tough!"

Mrs Green gave her a thoughtful look. “Why don’t you want her to work?” she asked.

Sam said, “If she goes out to work in the evenings, I’ll have to go to Dad’s.”

“Is that bad?” asked Mrs Green.

Sam told her that sometimes her dad worked late shifts. Then, she would have to go to a friend’s house.

“And is that bad?” asked Mrs Green.

Sam pointed out that although she liked her friends, she didn’t want to live in their houses half the time.

"My mum made us move into this flat without Dad, and now she'd rather serve dinners in a restaurant than stay at home with me," Sam complained.

"My whole life is horrible, and nobody cares!"

Mrs Green smiled and patted Sam's knee. "My old gran used to have an expression for how you're feeling today," she said. "She used to call it 'going down the garden to eat worms.' Everyone does it sometimes." She poured some more tea. "Of course, it doesn't do to feel sorry for yourself for too long, though," she added. "I try to look on the bright side as much as I can."

Sam groaned. How could she look on the bright side when there wasn't one?

Mrs Green put one cube of sugar in her tea, and another in her mouth. "I'll tell you what," she said, cheerfully. "I'll show you a game my old gran once showed me. Would you like that?"

Sam nodded, gloomily. She was only being polite. The last thing she wanted to do right now was play games, let alone ones that were a billion years old.

Chapter Three

The Blue Game

Mrs Green said, "Look around the room, and try to remember all the blue things." Sam looked around.

To a
Special
Gran

"Now, close your eyes," said Mrs Green, "and tell me all the things you saw that were red." Sam frowned. She couldn't remember anything that was red. She opened her eyes again.

"That's not fair!" Sam protested. "You told me to look for blue things. What was the point in that?"

Mrs Green said, "The point is, if you're only looking for blue, you don't even notice red."

"So?"

"So if you only look at the bad things in your life, you stop noticing the good things."

Sam accepted another slice of strawberry tart, and bit into it thoughtfully.

"This tart is good," she remarked.

Mrs Green was delighted. "That's the spirit!" she cried. "What else is good?"

Scrap put his paw on Sam's knee, and eyed the tart in her hand, hopefully.

"Scrap's good," Sam said, with a grin.

"What else?" asked Mrs Green.

Sam considered. "I don't know," she said, at last.

Mrs Green said, "What about your mum getting a job? Can you see any good things that might come out of that?"

"We'd have more money, I suppose," said Sam. "Perhaps we could have a holiday. That would be good."

She finished her strawberry tart and let Scrap lick her fingers. “But I still don’t want Mum to work in the evenings,” she said. “I can’t see any good in that.”

"You could always come here if your parents were both busy," Mrs Green suggested.

Sam was feeling much happier. By the time she went home, she was really keen for her mother to get a job. In fact, she could hardly wait.

Love's Sweet Scent

Chapter Four

The Garden

A few days later, Mrs Summerday got a phone call from the manager of The Garden Restaurant, asking her to come for an interview. Sam waited at home with her fingers crossed.

But as soon as her mother got back, Sam could tell that she hadn't got the job. She dropped her bag on the sofa and flopped into an armchair.

"It's hopeless," she told Sam. "I'll never get a job." She kicked off her shoes. "I've got no experience and no skills. I'm no good at anything."

Sam said, "Mrs Green calls that 'going down the garden to eat worms.' She says it's better to look on the bright side if you can."

"What bright side?" sighed her mum.

Sam said, "I know this new game that might cheer you up."

Mrs Summerday said the last thing she felt like doing was playing games. She was too old for games. But Sam told her it was a game for all ages – Mrs Green learned it from her old gran – and you couldn't get much older than that!

Sam played the blue game with her mum. After that, she helped her mum to notice all the things she was good at, like looking after Sam, finding out amazing facts, and reading stories so they seemed to come alive. Her mum cheered up a bit, but she still couldn't see anything good about not being able to get a job. Neither could Sam.

Then, the very next day, a job in the library was advertised.

"This one is made for you!" cried Sam.

"It's a good thing I didn't get any of those other jobs after all," said her mother. "I'd much rather work in the library."

The librarian knew Mrs Summerday because she was always visiting the library. She knew more about books than anyone else who applied. She knew how to choose them and use them. But most important of all, she loved books. The librarian gave her the job.

Sam and her mum decided to celebrate by going out for a meal. They both wanted to invite Mrs Green. They went round to her house.

"Guess what?" Sam said excitedly, as soon as Mrs Green came to the door. "Mum's got a job in the library!"

Mrs Green was delighted. "That's great news!" she cried.

"We'd like you to join us for a celebration," said Mrs Summerday. "We're going to The Garden Restaurant."

"But we won't be eating worms!" said Sam.

The Garden Restaurant
The Garden Restaurant
MENU